BRITAIN IN OLD PHOTOGRAPHS

LOWESTOFT

I A N   G .   R O B B

ALAN SUTTON PUBLISHING LIMITED

Alan Sutton Publishing Limited
Phoenix Mill · Far Thrupp · Stroud
Gloucestershire · GL5 2BU

First published 1995

Cover photographs: (Front) London Road South, pock-marked with shrapnel damage, April 1916; (Back) the demise of Beach Stone Place, December 1936.

British Library Cataloguing in Publication Data.
A catalogue record for this book is available from the British Library.

ISBN 0-7509-0854-8

Typeset in 9/10 Sabon.
Typesetting and origination by
Alan Sutton Publishing Limited.
Printed in Great Britain by
Ebenezer Baylis, Worcester.

Adam Adams, Mayor of Lowestoft, 1890/1, 1896/7 and 1907/8. He is best remembered for being drenched (twice) during a demonstration of the first steam-driven water pump for the local fire services in front of the Royal Hotel.

Contents

The bandstand, South Pier Pavilion, *c.* 1908. Bandmaster Holland is conducting a local band on a pleasant summer's day. The bandstand survived until the last war, when it was destroyed by bombing. It was photographed by Christopher Wilson.

Introduction

Lowestoft is the most easterly town in the British Isles. Until about 1800 it was a small fishing community consisting of one main thoroughfare perched on top of cliffs facing the North Sea. Its length was about 1 mile, commencing at Gallows Score (now Cart Score) and finishing at 'South End' (roughly where St Peter's Street and the High Street now converge). This thoroughfare had on its western, landward side a collection of lanes, while on the eastern, seaward side footpaths, known locally as 'scores', led down the face of the cliff to the Denes. Until the nineteenth century there was no harbour. Vessels landing goods at Lowestoft had them brought ashore by small boat, or the ships themselves were dragged up on the beach and their merchandise, usually fish, was sold in the open.

The town was never very large; the population was only about 2,000 by 1801. However, for its size, it had achieved considerable fame as a naval community of importance. The Dutch thought it worthwhile to do battle off its shores in 1665. Nautical worthies of the calibre of Sir Thomas Allin, Sir John Ashby, Vice-Admiral James Mighell and Captain Thomas Arnold were native to the town or lived here at one time or another. In the Napoleonic wars Lowestoft was one of many coastal towns to have batteries of cannon stationed in its vicinity, should invasion occur.

For centuries fish, especially the herring, provided the staple economy of the town. Lowestoft as a health resort, however, has come into being only within the last two centuries. From the 1760s the town gained a reputation as a health-restoring watering place. The gentry were advised to 'take the cure' on this part of the coast and Lowestoft in particular. It was during this period that the Lowestoft China Factory was founded. Built in Bell Lane and later extended to what became Factory Lane, it produced a variety of wares using locally dug clay. Its closure in around 1803 is said to have been caused by the seizure by the French of an important consignment bound for the continent, causing financial problems for the factory.

After 1815, when the Napoleonic Wars ended, the town continued to prosper. The London turnpike had already been constructed and new ventures such as the Bath House and Marine Terrace continued to attract visitors. In 1830 Lowestoft gained its first bridge. By the middle of that decade the town had almost doubled in population. But it was the vision of one man which transformed the town into something like its present state.

Sir Samuel Morton Peto, railway entrepreneur and MP for Norwich, saw the potential of Lowestoft as a port and as a resort of some eminence. It has now almost become a local legend how, for the small sum of £200, Peto bought a strip of sandy waste just south of the bridge and turned this windswept, desolate site into what became known as the New Town Estate. Linking the village of Kirkley to the town of Lowestoft, this spectacular venture had as its centre-piece the impressive Wellington Esplanade. In its day it was one of the finest terraced buildings on the east coast.

As to his plans for a port, Peto took over the existing harbour, then in financial trouble, and expanded it in size and scope. This enabled vessels to sail through Lowestoft to Norwich, thereby avoiding the heavy duties demanded by the rival port of Great Yarmouth. When the railway reached Lowestoft, it provided communication links not only with the Midlands but with the south and, importantly, with London. The boast that Lowestoft fish could be delivered fresh into the markets of the Midlands within twenty-four hours of being landed enhanced the reputation of the port. For a hundred years the railway played an important part in the prosperity of the town. It contributed to the quality of life in the locality, bringing people to the area and in return distributing the produce of Lowestoft throughout the country.

The town is not without its artistic connections. Two of the most eminent are Benjamin Britten, the composer, born in 1913 in Kirkley Cliff Road and George Davison, the celebrated photographer, pioneer of the secessionist movement in pictorial photography, and philanthropist, born in 1855 in Marine Parade. Other worthies include Charles Dickens, who stayed in the town and at Blundeston, George Borrow, who lived for a time at Oulton Broad, and Edward Fitzgerald, who was a regular visitor. The proudest claim to literary fame is that Lowestoft was the port at which Joseph Conrad first set foot on English soil and, more importantly, introduced Conrad to the English language.

The present century has had a marked effect on Lowestoft. The dramatic aftermath of two world wars brought much desolation. Because of the town's location as the most easterly area of population in England, it was the first target of enemy aircraft en route from Germany. There were regular attempts to destroy its naval and ship-building potential. Between 1940 and 1944 many areas of the town were laid to waste.

Urban expansion and the decline of the railway has affected the area considerably. As with other large towns, the motor vehicle has been the cause of many new routes churning through the environment, ruining much of its personality.

But we have our memories and through the medium of photography we can still savour what the town was like not so many years ago.

THE TOWN

*The two major industries of Lowestoft at the turn
of the century were leisure and fishing. This
photograph shows the resort, in the shape of the
Yacht Basin, and the Fish Market. The tower on
the left was called the Mount and was used as a
lookout for vessels returning to port.*

The junction of High Street and Compass Lane, c. 1896. This was the old town centre before Peto came to Lowestoft. The Star of Hope was one of many public houses around the Town Hall which disappeared with the widening of the street in 1898.

High Street, c. 1896. A very narrow thoroughfare, parts of it dated back to the sixteenth century. On the right, the tall structure is the rectory, built in the 1870s. Further up is Arnold House. The houses on the left were all pulled down when the street was widened.

Old Nelson Street, 1960s. This was part of the original Battery Green. Before the building of the fish market the beach came up to this point. In the foreground is the Battery Green car-park.

Crypt Steps, High Street, 1930s. Under many of the shops around the Town Hall there is evidence that before the Reformation there had been a religious establishment on the site. Some of these crypt cellars have been filled in over the years but a few survive, notably opposite the Town Hall itself.

Rant Score, the main thoroughfare down to the Denes from the old town, 1960s. The houses were demolished in the 1970s and part of the site was included in the extension of the Birds Eye food factory.

Mariners Score, *c.* 1905. It is a scene that until recent times had changed little; the archway remains, as does the large building, which is now the Ashlea Boys' Club. To the left of the archway once stood the old Swan Inn, used by Cromwell as his headquarters in 1643.

Duke's Head Street, looking east towards Rant Score and the High Street, 1950s. Originally known as Blue Anchor Lane, it was a street with historical connections. John Wesley held his meetings here on his visits to the town. It is regrettable that very little of Duke's Head Street survived the clearances of the 1960s.

St Peter's Chapel from the corner of Duke's Head Street and Chapel Street, 1950s. The church was built in 1833 as a chapel-at-ease to St Margaret's.

Factory Street, Lowestoft

Factory Street, *c.* 1903. This rare view shows the old bottle kiln of the Lowestoft China Factory, which was situated between Crown Street (originally Bell Lane) and Factory Street. The factory was established by Philip Walker, Obediah Aldred, Robert Williams and Robert Browne a year after Hewlin Luson of Gunton Hall built a temporary kiln on his estate in 1756. The clay used was a local type discovered near Corton. The photograph shows how the factory expanded piecemeal, until its closure in 1803. Remains of pottery and pottery moulds were discovered between 1902 and 1904 and also in the 1960s, when parts of the site were cleared. Part of the kiln site itself was included in what became the Winsor and Newton brush factory in 1947.

Lowestoft's original cast-iron swing bridge, seen from the south side looking towards Commercial Road, early 1860s. The bridge was opened in 1830 and stood for over sixty years, until replaced in 1897. The trees are those of the Grove Estate.

The southern approach to the second swing bridge, 1959. Opened in 1897, this bridge did sterling service until 1969, when its mechanism broke down, cutting the town in half. Craske's and the building on the right were demolished to make way for a replacement bridge. Note the semaphore (centre), which was used to inform shipping when the bridge was open or closed.

Pier Terrace with St John's Church and the Harbour Hotel, *c.* 1870. Among the businesses in the terrace were W.B. Farrett, chemist, and Robert Turner, picture-frame maker, over whose shop was a photographic studio.

St John's Church, London Road South, *c.* 1861. It was built in 1853 by the Lucas Brothers for Sir Morton Peto, at a cost of £5,600. The church served the rapidly growing population south of the bridge. This early photograph was taken by James Saunders of Kirkley, who opened a studio in around 1857.

The Infirmary, Cage Green, early 1860s. Built in 1839, on the site of a cage used to detain felons and drunkards, the Infirmary replaced an earlier hospital in Crown Street. Over the years the Infirmary was enlarged, but in the 1870s a new hospital was erected in Milton Road, and later St Margaret's National School was built on the site. Cage Green was on the corner of Fly Close (now the bottom end of Park Road) and Dove Lane. It became known as Infirmary Green and later St Margaret's Plain. In the photograph, the cottages on the left lead into Fly Close and Mariners Lane. Dove Lane is on the right.

The North End, early 1860s. This is a view from the traditional drying ground of the North Denes, with the fishing nets laid out to catch the early morning sun. The backs and gardens of the residences in the High Street overlook the North Sea. These fine terraces were interspersed with alcoves and summer-houses, running down to the foot of the cliffs. There, buildings associated with the fishing industry, mainly smoke-houses, extended the length of the old town. The scene is probably very much as it would have been a hundred years before. This was the heart of seventeenth-century and eighteenth-century Lowestoft and was where its naval heroes lived and worked. This photograph includes the homes of the Allins, the Mighells and, of course, the Arnolds, who lived in the first of the large houses to the right. This scene had been described some years before in the *Universal British Directory* as 'the noblest and most beautiful appearance from the sea of any town upon the coast'. Many of the houses on the cliff top dated from the late seventeenth and eighteenth century, some hiding earlier internal structures dating back to the sixteenth century. This rebuilding was the result of periodical fires and especially the disastrous fire of March 1645, which broke out in one of the smoke-houses below and spread to houses in the High Street itself.

Old Nelson Street from Battery Green in the 1860s, showing a mixture of house styles dating from the eighteenth century onwards. The towers are those of the Congregational Church, erected in 1852. The woman on the right is standing outside Bow House, which had been a public house for troops on the Southern Battery during the Napoleonic Wars.

J.A. Spargo, chemist and druggist, of Pier Terrace, mid-1870s. A chemist had been on this site since the 1860s and James Alfred Spargo had succeeded W.B. Farrett. It is possible that the gentleman seated in the carriage with the restless horse is Spargo himself.

High Street at the corner of Duke's Head Street, *c.* 1880. In the distance is the Town Hall, built in the 1850s on the site of the old Town Chamber. The older houses, dating from the previous two centuries, are beginning to make way for Victorian commercial properties on both sides of the street. Crane's jeweller's shop, the tall building on the left, was later to be joined by Geneva House, with its well-known clock. Regrettably this clock has now been replaced by something that looks like a cut-out. Further up on the same side is the Crown Hotel, which still looks much the same today. Most of the properties on the right were owned by William Youngman, a brewer. Youngman's house dwarfs two interesting eighteenth-century shops. Gurney's Bank, once the Star Hotel and later Barclays Bank, nestles next to Youngman's abode.

Kirkley Cliff, *c*. 1880. This sweeping view is from the junction of Cliff Road, looking north towards Peto's Wellington Esplanade. These later houses reflect the continuation of Peto's dream (see page 46, top). The furthest south that Peto reached was South Lodge (right), although a footpath linked Pakefield with Lowestoft along the cliff top. South Lodge later became a preparatory school, one of whose pupils was the young Benjamin Britten. In this early morning photograph a young lady (left) looks inquisitively out of a first-floor window towards the camera.

Warren House, Gunton Denes, 1890s. Clay for the china factory was washed here and flint was ground for the making of porcelain. The house was later divided into three. Picnickers used to obtain fresh water from here and the spring still gushes forth today. The Denes beyond the house were used as training grounds for the Rifle Volunteers.

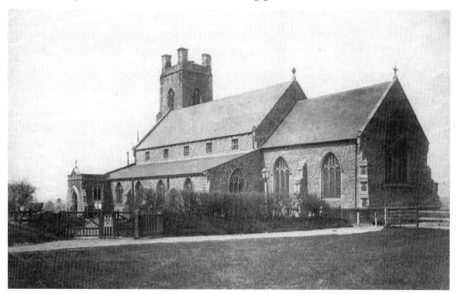

St Peter's Church, Kirkley, *c.* 1893. A church has stood on this hilltop overlooking the Ham since before the Norman Conquest. Neglected in the seventeenth century, this church was restored first in 1750. The present building dates from the 1880s.

High Street, 1896. H. Bunn, tobacconist, is on the right. Both sides of the street were built on very early foundations. The house on the left with the overhanging first floor was then a public house. Today it is an antiques shop. It dates back to the fifteenth century and is the oldest building in the town.

This proud owner sits in his 1904 de Dion-Bouton, parked in the precincts of the swing bridge. A reliable car, this model proved very popular until it was succeeded by the Ford Model 'T' of 1908.

Wilmington House, Kirkley Park Road, *c.* 1905. Built in 1891, it was the residence of John Wilton, timber merchant, whose works were in Belvedere Road. The house later accommodated the first St Mary's Convent. It is now a nursing home.

The cemetery gatehouse and lodge, *c.* 1910. Lowestoft Cemetery was opened in 1887. In later years trees obscured the view of the chapel. The railings were removed during the last war.

Scottish girls on the Fish Market, *c.* 1905. These girls came to Lowestoft for the herring season and worked on the pickling plots in the town. They were always active even during their leisure time, and as proof of an old saying that their fingers were never idle, four of the five here are merrily knitting.

North Quay, showing the Great Eastern Railway works and the Customs and Excise buildings, *c.* 1905. The harbour master's house (centre) was destroyed in a bombing raid in February 1941.

A smack (LT245) waits to go through the swing bridge from Lake Lothing to the outer harbour, c. 1905. The view is from the South Quay.

The Fish Market, looking towards the Trawl Basin and the entrance to the Waveney Dock, c. 1905. The Mount is on the right.

St Margaret's, the parish church of Lowestoft, 1911. The present edifice dates from 1483 and is an enlargement of an earlier structure, of which only the tower survives. The original community lived around the church, but sometime early in the town's history the population moved to its present, more convenient location, on the cliff top in the area which later became the High Street.

Sparrow's Nest, c. 1909. Originally a summer residence for Robert Sparrow of Worlingham, the estate was bought by the town in 1897 and turned into pleasure gardens. During the last war it was taken over by the Naval Patrol Service, which extended the house and gave it a flat roof. The old house was demolished in the 1960s.

Rough seas pound the South Pier, *c.* 1910. The viciousness of the North Sea along this coast is amply demonstrated in this view taken from the South Beach. The light on the pier head is one of a pair built for Peto in the 1840s.

Savage & Son, on the corner of London Road North and Waveney Road, 1890s. The Savages were family butchers who had taken over the business of C. Burton in about 1893 or 1894. By 1902 father and son seem to have parted company. Eventually Tuttle's took over these premises and others on the block, and the corner became known as Tuttle's Corner. The tower over the shop was destroyed in a roof fire in 1964.

The fire at Lowestoft Net Works, Clapham Road, June 1907. It was described in the local paper as 'spectacular'; a breeze fanned the flames, which were made all the more fierce by the presence of oil stored in barrels on the premises. No lives were lost.

Lowestoft No. 1 tram en route for the Central Railway Station, *c.* 1910. Posing for the camera on a cold winter's day, the tram has stopped in front of the Convalescent Home on the corner of Yarmouth Road and the High Street. The conductor may be Frederick Mitchell.

A Brooke four-cylinder tourer outside the post office in London Road North, 1905. This example of Lowestoft workmanship was about to commence a test run for the GPO.

A tram waits to return to Lowestoft at the tram terminus, Pakefield, before 1910. At one time the main road used to turn to the right, up Pakefield Street. A coal cart stands outside the Tramway Hotel, indicating that the driver has popped in for a quick one.

On 1 June 1914 six members of the 1st Troop Carlton Colville Sea Scouts were drowned in a boating accident on the River Waveney. One boy survived. On the day of the funeral a large turnout watched the procession of horse-drawn hearses travel from Oulton Broad to Carlton Colville churchyard. The Bishop of Norwich conducted the service.

Floral tributes on the graves of the sea scouts.

Workmen keep an eye on the sea defences at the base of Kirkley Cliff, *c*. 1930.

A family group in Barnard's Yard, 1917. Barnard's Yard, also known as Barrett's Yard, was situated behind 112 and 113 High Street. Like many other similar locations in the town, it was probably built around a spring or well, served at this date by a pump similar to one in Duke's Head Street. The site of the yard is now Artillery Way.

RNLI lifeboat *Hugh Taylor* outside its shed on the Denes, about to depart for Kessingland, 1931. No longer needed at Lowestoft, she was transferred further down the coast to Kessingland, where she replaced the *St Paul*. There, the *Hugh Taylor* remained until 1936, when the Kessingland lifeboat station closed down. The old shed in this photograph became a workshop for a haulage company, until it was pulled down in the Beach Village clearances of the 1960s.

A proud crew stand beside Crossley BJ–7065, which is painted in the livery of the Lowestoft Cooperative Society, 1920s. The design of the vehicle, and its acetylene lights, suggest that this was an ex-RAF lorry.

A London & Midland Scottish Railway float in a carnival procession, 1920s. The LMS was one of the two main railways serving Lowestoft. It connected the area with the Midlands and its markets. It also brought in the army of Scottish fisher girls.

The 'George Elizabeth' float under construction in the Eastern Coach Works factory in Eastern Way, April 1937. It was made for the procession held to celebrate the coronation of George VI in May of that year.

The finished vehicle complete with its attendants, May 1937. The photograph was taken outside the coach works by Swains of Norwich.

RNLI lifeboat *Agnes Cross*, *c.* 1938. This was Lowestoft's first motor lifeboat and the last to be based on the Norfolk and Suffolk design. It was the gift of Mrs Agnes Cross of London and saw service between 1921 and 1939, during which time the crew saved over two hundred lives.

Craftsmen at the United Automobile bodywork factory, Laundry Lane, *c.* 1930. Founded in 1920, it originally constructed bus bodies for ex-military vehicles and later for new chassis. In 1931 United became Eastern Counties Omnibuses and in 1936 the coach works became a separate branch of Eastern Counties.

HMS *Godetia* bedecked with flags, 1930s. She succeeded HMS *Halcyon* in 1933 as the fisheries protection vessel for this area. She survived the war and continued in service until the 1950s. She is seen moored in the Yacht Basin. The event in which she is taking part could be either the silver jubilee of George V in 1935 or the coronation of George VI in 1937. Godetia Court, in the north of the town, was named after her.

Pakefield Terminus, looking from Pakefield Street towards Stradbrooke Road, 1963. The old toll-booth stands on the corner (left). The illustrator Michael Foreman lived there as a young boy. Two Lowestoft Corporation buses stand ready to return to town, almost in the same place as the trams stood all those years before. Note the old gas lamp in the foreground (right).

RNLI lifeboat *Frederick Edward Crick* moored in the Hamilton Dock, 1963. This was the vessel's first year of duty. She replaced the *Michael Stephens* and was herself replaced in the 1980s.

St John's Church, late 1950s. The clock had been added in 1887. The cinema (left) is the Palace, which was one of the first purpose-built cinemas in Lowestoft.

The dredger *Lake Lothing* working in the Herring Basin, 1960. Built in 1955 at the Leith yard of Henry Robb, it was 156 ft long and had a capacity of 800 tons of mud. It was estimated that annually it removed some 17,000 tons from the harbour.

Station Square, looking south towards the bridge and St John's, late 1950s. The Corporation bus shelter, traffic-lights and islands are in the middle of what is now a pedestrianized area.

London Road North looking north from the same vantage point, late 1950s. At this date it was the main A12 trunk road but note the lack of traffic! The sign over the pavement belonged to Smiths, furnishers (right).

The huge Hensen crane on the South Quay, 1962. Weighing some 200 tons, it was built to off-load material bound for the first Sizewell power station. Moored alongside is LT188 *Tritonia*, looking more like a little toy than a full-sized ship. The site is now part of SLP Ltd, a company specializing in building rigs for the oil industry.

London Road North, 1963. The photograph shows the only two shops on the Arcade site to have escaped destruction in 1943. However, Walker's Stores and the *Lowestoft Journal* office finally surrendered to the bulldozer later in the 1960s and their replacements were built in alignment with the other shops.

London Road North, 1963. This was originally the London turnpike, built in the late eighteenth century, and a tollbooth stood on the piece of land to the left. Camp's Antiques, destroyed in the last war, was the last building on the site. The two shops on the right were pulled down in 1993 and Artillery Way now cuts across this scene.

L.H. Mitchell General Stores, on the corner of Oulton Road and Hollingsworth Road, *c.* 1950. In the doorway stands Lilian Hannah Mitchell with Leslie and Linda, two young relatives. The shop remained a general store until the early 1990s.

The original coastguard station, Newcombe Road, photographed just before the Beach Village clearances, 1960s. Jaqueline Rose and David Field stand in the doorway. Pryce's warehouse is in the background.

The Yacht Basin, looking towards the swing bridge and Pier Terrace, summer 1959. Crossing the bridge on its way to Pakefield is one of our sadly missed Corporation buses. As far as I can make out, it is one of the well-known 1946 vintage AEC Regents, the bodies of which were made locally at the Eastern Coach Works. Only a few years after this photograph was taken this fine view was marred by the incursion of the tall grain silo built in Commercial Road.

Section Two

THE RESORT

The Royal Norfolk and Suffolk Yacht Club, Royal
Plain, c. 1904. Designed by G. & F. Skipper and
built in 1902, it was officially opened the
following year by Lord Claude Hamilton of the
Great Eastern Railway Company.

Bath House, Battery Green, *c.* 1859. Built in 1824, by the date of this photograph it was being run by a Mrs Peters and supplied hot and cold seawater baths to the Victorian gentry.

Bath House, just before its demolition in the 1960s. This part of Battery Green had been renamed Hamilton Road. Like many others, these two buildings were swept away with the construction of the Beach Industrial Estate.

Marine Terrace, London Road, *c*. 1859. Built by James Fisher, these houses had pleasant gardens leading to Battery Green.

Sparrow's Nest Gardens, 1906. This scene encapsulates the pleasures of taking tea in the open air in the gentility and serenity of an Edwardian summer. The upper windows at this corner of the house have survived, but are hidden in the fabric of the present structure.

Wellington Esplanade, early 1860s. The jewel in Peto's New Town Estate, this elegant terrace was designed by John Thomas, Peto's brilliant architect. Michael Barrett's photograph also shows the newly laid out gardens belonging to the houses. A boy sits on what had been waste ground.

The Esplanade with Wellington Gardens on the left, mid-1860s. Also shown here is Victoria Terrace. Behind the group of boys stands the large house demolished in the 1950s. Peto House now stands on the site of this building.

The entrance to the South Pier, 1860s. Built on the outer pier in the 1840s, it included the gracefully designed Reading Room; this was the first of three structures on the pier and can be seen in the distance. In 1885 it was destroyed by fire, along with part of the pier.

The Esplanade, early 1860s. The remains of the sandy waste can be seen behind the seated boy. Eventually a promenade was completed, leading from the South Pier to Pakefield. The photograph is by Michael Barrett.

The Royal Hotel, *c.* 1890. It was built by the Lucas Brothers as part of Peto's plan to make Lowestoft a grander watering-place than before, and was recognized as one of the finest hotels in England. It succeeded in attracting many distinguished people and lived up to its name when royalty, in the person of Prince Albert, actually did stay here. Regrettably the hotel was demolished in 1973. The site remained a grassy waste until the East Point Pavilion was built there; it opened in May 1993. One of the sets of royal coats of arms decorating the hotel entrance is now housed in the pavilion.

The Esplanade, looking south past Parade Road South towards Kirkley Cliff, mid-1890s. Most of the buildings were either hotels or guest-houses. Standing guard, to the left, is one of two statues of the sea god Triton. Apsley House and Blenheim (just right of the statue) became at one time the Ministry of Agriculture, Fisheries, and Food and was the only block demolished. The Hatfield Private Hotel (far right) is still in business over a hundred years later. In the distance (left of the statue) is South Lodge.

Royal Plain, looking towards the South Pier Pavilion, 1910. The pavilion was built between 1885 and 1891. Here, the entrance to the pier has been altered but is still recognizable from some sixty years before (see page 47, top). Parked in front of the Yacht Club are two motor cars, both chauffeur driven. The car on the left is a veteran Lanchester of 1907, with tiller steering. It is thought that this vehicle may have belonged to Howard Hollingsworth of Bourne & Hollingsworth fame, who lived on Gunton Cliff. The other car is a Ford Model 'T' from about 1908. A wagonette can be seen at the bottom right; this vehicle was the predecessor of the motor charabanc. It was normally a two-horse-driven affair, and was used for taking holiday-makers for trips into the countryside.

The Royal Plain from the tower of the South Pier Pavilion, 1959. The Royal Hotel is on the left and the spire of St John's is behind the Palace Cinema. The Palace was built on the site of the Royal Hotel stables. For some years it was a circus, until it became a cinema in 1913. On the right is the Royal Norfolk and Suffolk Yacht Club.

After suffering from years of neglect because of the war, the South Pier Pavilion was demolished in May 1954. It was replaced by a new pavilion in 1956.

The beach at Pakefield, 1930s. This scene, with bathers, tents and beach huts, would suggest that the sands could be serene all the year round. For those who lived there the tale would be very different; Cliff Road, in the background, was to suffer serious damage from erosion.

Pakefield, seen from the caravan camp, thirty years on. By now the sea has scooped away land up to the church and in receding has left a pleasant little sandy bay, which has expanded over the years.

Victoria bathing chalets, Kirkley Cliff, 1930s. Above the chalets are the Victoria Mansions, built in 1897.

The bathing-pool, c. 1926. This was supplied by seawater from its own groyne just off the beach. It was part of the Recreational Grounds laid out on the North Denes in 1925, on land that had been the town allotments. The complex consisted of bathing-pool, model-yacht pond and sports grounds. The latter included a cricket pitch and tennis courts. The Admiralty took over during the last war and used the area for training. It is now a caravan camp.

Looking across the Children's Corner to the South Pier Pavilion, 1963. The pavilion was the last of three such structures built on the pier. Opened in 1956 by the Duke of Edinburgh, it had the attraction of a tower. The two previous pavilions had catered for more sedate times, but this new one drew in a different clientele; it boasted a dance floor, theatre and amusements, in keeping with the faster pace of the postwar era. Alas, it was also to be short-lived, for in the late 1980s the pavilion was demolished as being 'unsafe'. It has not been replaced and the pier looks quite bare. The only vestige of its former glory survives at the entrance to the pier.

Donkeys had been giving children rides on or near the Wellington Gardens for well over sixty years when this photograph was taken in the early 1950s. They disappeared when Fred Jones, Lowestoft's last donkey man, retired, to become, like so many, yet another fading memory.

The boating lake and gardens, 1950s. After 1945 the Borough Council decided to demolish most of the remaining houses on the Esplanade and replace them with gardens and amenities. These became a boon to the boarding-houses in Marine Parade.

Miniature steam locomotive *Sonia*, 1961. One of the popular postwar attractions on the Esplanade was the miniature railway next to the Royal Hotel. For *9d* passengers were treated to three circuits of the track. The train driver for many years was Albert Reynolds. The track was removed in the early 1970s and *Sonia* was last heard of in private hands in Scotland. Who the young boy is, I regret I have no clue.

Section Three

THE FISHING
INDUSTRY

Fisher girls, mid-1920s. Standing among barrels
of herring on the North Denes, these girls worked
in the open in all weathers, with little visible
protection. Their fingers were bandaged, however,
to protect them from the brine and the raw salt.

The Fish Market, *c.* 1905. Edward Thain also had a fish restaurant by the bridge. The fish here was iced and packed in wooden 'kits', which were moved by large barrows similar to the one on the right. This was a style of barrow used until recent times.

LT203 *John and Norah* newly fitted out and ready for her maiden voyage in 1911.

Processing and packing herring, Denmark Road, 1920s. The railway system was essential for transporting fish to the home markets. At the height of the season even railway sidings were taken up as pickling plots.

The trawler LT295 *Suffolk Maid*, *c.* 1960. Photographed by Ernest Graystone, it is passing the dredger *Lake Lothing* on its way out to sea. The *Suffolk Maid* was built by Richards, one of many famous shipbuilders once established in the port, and was owned by Small & Co. Launched in 1959, she fished out of Lowestoft until 1970, when she was sold to Aberdeen and renamed *Anna Christina*.

Painters on board LT511, *c.* 1914. An important part of the ship was its name and registration number, but photographs of them being painted on the hull of a vessel seem to be scarce. As with all aspects of fishing, danger lurked here, and it was not unusual for a poor soul to fall from his painter's cradle into the murky dock.

Unloading fish on to the dock side, *c.* 1904. Taken from the boats in baskets, the fish was usually displayed in the open on the floor of the market.

Lowestoft's mighty fishing fleet in 1912. The vessels are moored in the Herring Basin. A barge can be seen transporting coals to the steam drifters. These drifters gained the nickname of 'Woodbines' because of the shape of their funnels. Once steam had proven its worth, they quickly took over from the older sailing smacks. Judging by the lack of Scottish boats this photograph was taken out of the herring season. The scene would dramatically change when drifters from other English and Scottish ports would be crammed into the basin.

The crew of the smack *Welcome*, moored in the Trawl Basin, pose at ease for the camera, *c.* 1905.

Young girls at the Vigilant Fishing Company's yard, Whapload Road, *c.* 1927. Back row, left to right: Edie Winter, Ethel Winter, Corra Rouse, Gladys Page, Emily Meades, Hannah Coleman, Millie Winter. Front row: Nellie Winter, Edie Oldman, Barbara Coleman.

An old salt gazes on the smacks moored in the Trawl Basin, *c.* 1903. The market and its activities were a favourite haunt for holiday-makers and locals alike.

Trawl Basin, *c.* 1920. Although greatly reduced in number, the sailing smacks survived beyond the First World War and into the 1930s. Many were owned by individual owner-skippers. Among the vessels here is the *Children's Friend*.

Beeton's Net Works, Beach Village, 1960s. This village housed a vast array of supporting trades to the fishing industry. As well as the net works, there were smokehouses, chandlers, stores and, of course, public houses. The site was cleared for the Beach Industrial Estate.

Loading fish, 1950s. Road transport took over from rail for the delivery of fish. Here, the fish is given a final coating of ice before being loaded into insulated road containers.

The tug *Lound* taking LT58 *Boston Pegasus* through the swing bridge, 1959. The *Lound* was one of a series of tugs designed for working between the outer harbour and Lake Lothing. The *Boston Pegasus* belonged to the Boston Deep Sea Fisheries, which was prominent in Lowestoft and several other ports on the east coast. The sight of a vessel going through the bridge has always been an attraction, especially to holidaymakers, who can be seen here standing on the north side of the bridge. The building immediately behind them was demolished when the present bridge was constructed.

Off to the fishing grounds, 1940s. The drifter LT200 *Marshall Pak* and her sister ships make their way towards the golden shoals of herring. Each year from 1936 to 1966, with only a break forced by the last war, the Prunier Trophy was presented by Madame Simone Prunier of the Prunier Restaurant in London. The winner of this coveted trophy was the boat that caught the largest number of herring at one time and landed them at either Lowestoft or Great Yarmouth. Lowestoft boats won the trophy more times than any other port. The competition was abandoned in 1966; after many years of overfishing the herring had almost disappeared from the North Sea. This classic photograph was taken by Ernest Graystone.

The steam drifter *Joe Chamberlain* entering the harbour, *c.* 1914.

LT225 *Kirkley* moored along the old Trawl Dock, 1959. In the 1950s there were only five steam drifters left. By the end of the decade those that remained had been converted to diesel. The *Kirkley*, shown here with its patched-up wooden hull, ended its career when it ran aground on the Scroby Sands in 1963.

Scottish fisher girls, looking a bit mature by the 1950s. They were photographed by Ernest Graystone.

Trawler LT42 *Bahama* passing through the swing bridge, 1959.

Filleting and packing hall, Explorator Ltd, Battery Green Road, 1956. The thin young man handling the labels or 'tallies' as they were known, is Basil King. In the white coat and sporting a flat cap is the foreman Donny Pretty, and behind him is Chy Manthorpe, fish buyer. On the right, facing young Basil and also wearing a cap, is Eddie Willis. The hall was situated near the corner of Suffolk Road, almost opposite the entrance to the Fish Market. Explorator pioneered insulated road transportation of fish in the early 1950s, though the business was taken over by the Ross Group in the mid-1960s. Ford Jenkins took the photograph.

A Bedford lorry in the green and white colours of A.E. Balls, *c.* 1949. This lorry was registered in 1946 and is seen here working on the Fish Market, carrying a load of empty fish boxes. Arthur Edward Balls had been carting fish since the 1920s and continued until the 1950s or so. He lived in Water Lane, where at one time he also garaged his vehicles. Road transport had taken over from rail fairly rapidly after the last war. A combination of increased rail freight charges and the availability of motor transport left over from the war, and no longer required by the armed forces, brought forth a new era in fish delivery. It was cheap, overnight and direct to the shop door from the fish market.

THE PEOPLE

Skipper Ernest 'Jumbo' Fiske. This portrait was
taken in the early 1960s by Ernest Graystone.
'Jumbo' was well respected and well liked in the
town. One of his achievements when he was
skipper of the Suffolk Warrior *was to win the*
Prunier Trophy in 1964. This was the final
successful year of the herring fishery. It is said
that his was one of the last catches of herring off
the Smith-Knoll lightship.

Lady Pleasance Smith, photographed by Henry Bevan in her 103rd year. Born in 1773, she was the daughter of Robert Reeve, a member of the eminent Lowestoft family. In 1796 she married Sir James Edward Smith, founder of the Linnean Society. A generous benefactor to the town, she was greatly mourned when she died in 1877. Lady Smith is buried with her husband in St Margaret's churchyard.

Mr Fred Jones, early 1890s. This is an early portrait of Lowestoft's well-known 'Donkey Man', who for many years gave rides to generations of children on the Esplanade.

A local character photographed by Boughton in 1903.

Dean Edward Lowry Henderson MA, *c.* 1911. He came to Lowestoft from Derby and was Rector of Lowestoft from 1910 to 1916. He left the town for Gloucester and later became Provost of St Mary's Cathedral, Edinburgh. He is buried in Salisbury Cathedral.

Revd Albert Darell Tupper-Carey, 1902. He was Rector of Lowestoft from 1902 to 1910 and is one of the best remembered incumbents of St Margaret's. He threw himself into the life of the town. In his time St Peter's Chapel was extended and he built St Andrew's Church in Roman Road. He sometimes accompanied the drifters on their journeys to the northern waters. His passion for fish was such that he was often seen cycling home from the Fish Market to the Rectory with herring, mackerel or plaice dangling from his handle-bars.

Revd Francis Cunningham MA, Rector of Pakefield from 1814 to 1855 and Vicar of Lowestoft from 1830 to 1860. He was born in 1785 and married Richenda Gurney of Earlham, Norwich, who was the sister of Elizabeth Fry. Cunningham was responsible for the Cunningham Schools in Pakefield and the High Street. He also introduced George Borrow to the charms of Lowestoft in 1832. He died in 1863, aged seventy-eight, and is buried in St Margaret's churchyard.

Thomas Elvin Thirtle, Mayor of Lowestoft from 1910 to 1912. He ran the family ironmonger's from the 1870s to the early years of this century. He was honorary Chief Fire Officer, churchwarden, town councillor and on numerous other committees including that of the local football team, as well as owning at least five fishing smacks, all named after flowers.

T.E. Thirtle standing outside his shop at 45 High Street, c. 1872. The shop was originally Chaston House, the residence of John Jex (c. 1688–1777), and George II stayed here in 1737. The little plaque over the doorway, bearing the town's old coat of arms, survived until the 1970s, when it disappeared.

Rose Lincoln, early 1880s. She was one of the Lincolns of Pakefield who were prominent in the local fishing at that time. The smack *John Lincoln* was named after a member of the family.

Samuel Capps, *c*. 1864. He was a sail maker by trade. The Capps originated from Kent and followed the fishing up the east coast, possibly as far as Grimsby. A branch of the family settled in Lowestoft at the beginning of the nineteenth century. From this line descended such diverse people as Robert Capps, smack owner, Alderman A. Brame Capps and Edmund Capps, the singer, who emigrated to Canada in 1906.

The first intake of children at Church Road Infants' School, 1896. The school was built to cater for the new homes then being built in the area. It was renamed St Margaret's Infant's School in around 1950.

Group one, St Andrew's School, c. 1905. St Andrew's Roman Hill Infants' was built in 1898 for 236 pupils. It is now an annex of Lowestoft College.

Robert Beattie Nicholson OBE. He was the first town clerk of the Borough of Lowestoft, in 1885. According to a lecture he gave in 1925, when he arrived from Carlisle, Lowestoft was just recovering from one of its many outbreaks of smallpox. He was a member of the Royal Commission on Coastal Erosion, and retired in the early 1920s.

Ivan Kittle as the King of Cadonia in the Lowestoft Amateur Operatic and Dramatic Society's production staged at the Marina Theatre, 5 May 1913. Until the rise of the cinema, such productions were very popular and were eagerly attended. *The King of Cadonia* was described as a lavish affair and according to the *Lowestoft Journal* 'no expense seems to have been spared' to give the audience an exciting evening.

Louie White as Princess Marie in *The King of Cadonia*. The Lowestoft Amateur Operatic and Dramatic Society was founded in 1911. The Marina Theatre was a popular favourite with such companies for holding extravaganzas until the late 1920s, when it became a cinema.

Elsie, one of the chorus line of the society's
1923 production of the light opera
Veronique.

Members of the society in the 1920s, reflecting the new influences in the theatre of the
day. This relaxed group is more reminiscent of the troupe in Priestley's *The Good
Companions*.

Charles Wilson, *c.* 1914. Wilson was the cook on the fishing smack *Research*. He was killed in June 1916 when the vessel was shelled by a German submarine.

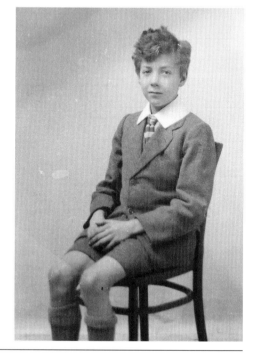

Edward Benjamin Britten, 1923. The portrait was taken by Christopher Wilson and young Benjamin is wearing the uniform of South Lodge Preparatory School, Kirkley Cliff. His father, Robert Britten, was a dentist with a practice in Kirkley Cliff Road. Above the waiting room, patients would be serenaded by Benjamin practising his scales on the piano. Some of his best-known works are *Albert Herring*, *Peter Grimes* and *The Young Person's Guide to the Orchestra*.

GER cup winners, 1911. Before the First World War churches, businesses, schools, and even streets had football teams of various ages and abilities.

1st Lowestoft (St Margaret's) Scouts, October 1913. Troops in the area competed for a flag, which was presented by the district commissioner. The first contest took place at Gunton Hall. St Margaret's won by the narrow margin of one mark. With the boys are Scoutmaster E.W. Capps and Assistant Scoutmaster Sydney Hall.

Buffalo Patrol and Lone Scouts, 1st Lowestoft Scouts, Whitsun 1915. This was to be the last summer camp at Herringfleet Hills for the duration of the war.

1st Lowestoft Scout Troop, August 1925. Summer camps continued after the war at Herringfleet and, despite a second break in the last war, are still being held.

Syd Mitchell standing windswept but in a happy mood among the streamers, July 1935. Towns up and down the country celebrated the silver jubilee of George V in June 1935. Lowestoft held its celebrations in July, which coincided with the golden jubilee of the town's borough status (1885).

Morton Road School netball team, 1924–6. Front row, left to right: Amy Smith, Sylvia Warren, Bessie Jones. Back row: Doris Stannard, Muriel Mullender (killed in an air-raid during the war), Vicky Manning, Ethel Rushmere.

George Coleman in his little 'Tin Ford', *c.* 1930. Built by his father, who also took the photograph, this was a unique pedal car. It was also the envy of the local children, who tended to tip up the car with poor young Georgie inside it.

There is something about this part of the coast that fascinates the literary world and leads its members to spend some time here. Such was the case of H. Rider Haggard, author of *King Solomon's Mines* and *She*, who lived at the Grange in Kessingland before the First World War. The photograph was taken in around 1912.

Church Road Girls' School Guide group on parade on Battery Green, 1920s. The fishing industry was never far away; stacked in the background are fish boxes, into which the herring were packed.

The crew of the steam hopper *Pioneer*, *c.* 1910. G. Crickmore, E. Hyard (?) and A. Howlett manned the vessel, which was built in 1886 to suck up the mud from the harbour. Owned by the GER, it was still working in the 1950s.

John Walter Brooke, Mayor of Lowestoft from 1912 to 1916. Brooke founded his engineering works in Adrian Road, building engines for general marine use. His first motor car was built in 1902 and up to the First World War Brooke concentrated on motor vehicles. Brooke's first love, however, was boats. In 1912 the shipyard at Oulton Broad was being developed and from 1914 the firm mainly produced marine engines and ships. This continued after the war, and Brooke's yard developed a reputation for building a variety of ships, civil and naval, of a very high standard.

Section Five

WARTIME

Sandringham Road, 25 April 1916. Sydney
Davey, his sister Annie and a young child, Robert
Mumford, lost their lives in this house.

In 1915 Lowestoft fell victim to Zeppelin attacks. As the airships passed over the town, the crews manually dropped their bombs over the side. However, more damage was done by bomb blast than by direct hits, as this photograph shows. It was taken after a raid in Kimberley Road in April of that year.

Another view of Kimberley Road after the same raid. Children gather around a shell crater at the rear of the same terraces. Zeppelin airships were at the mercy of the weather and tended to drop their bombs on the nearest populated area if they could not reach their targets. On this occasion no one was killed here.

Apsley and Blenheim boarding-houses on the Esplanade, after a Zeppelin raid, 1915.

The South Pier Pavilion was commandeered by the Navy and used as barracks. It also suffered in the 1915 attack. The photograph is by Christopher Wilson.

London Road South, from the junction of Freemantle Road (left) and looking towards Windsor Road, 25 April 1916. At around 4 am, a cruiser squadron consisting of *Der Flinger*, *Moltke* and *Van der Taan* shelled the town for twenty minutes. Four people were killed. This and the following eight photographs show some of the damage; here, the shops and houses are pock-marked with shrapnel damage. Although Lowestoft was the nearest sizeable British town to Germany, and despite its naval and engineering activities, defences here and at other east coast towns were inadequate. Perhaps the authorities did not think that the enemy would venture so close to land. Until May 1916 the port had very poor security against sea and air attack.

Ashby Road, 25 April 1916. No. 2 was hit by a shell, which smashed through one window and flew out of the other.

In Kent Road a 12 in shell crashed through thirteen houses and came to rest in the last one, without exploding. This last house is identified by the boy leaning against the garden wall (centre).

Edgar & Co., photographers, London Road South. Edgar Woodcock lived on the premises and narrowly escaped with his life when a large shell came through the upper storey of the building.

The rear of Edgar & Co. The shell went through the building, demolishing the rear, and continued its flight until it hit two houses in an adjoining road. The large glasshouse seen here was Edgar's photographic studio.

North End, Yarmouth Road. This house was located opposite the Belle Vue Park. When the shell hit the house, the owner was pinned down underneath the rubble and died when the house burst into flames. What was left of the building was reconstructed using some of the original material, and still stands today.

A few shells landed inland as far as Kirkley Run, destroying these newly built houses.

Cleveland Road, south Lowestoft, which, along with the neighbouring Windsor Road, received direct hits. Considering how many shells were fired into the town and the resulting damage, the death toll was very low.

Esplanade, next to the Royal Hotel. A shell exploded inside the house, splitting it almost in two.

Sentries on duty at Mutford Lock, Oulton Broad, during the First World War. Behind is the Wherry Hotel, built in the late 1890s. This unusual photograph of such a sensitive strategic location must have been taken with the knowledge of those on guard. There were only four road bridges to and from the island of Lothingland at the time: the harbour bridge at Lowestoft, Mutford Lock linking Lake Lothing and the Broads, St Olave's Bridge over the Waveney, and the bridge linking Southtown and Great Yarmouth.

These two converted trawlers, moored along the South Quay, are on minesweeping duties, c. 1942. The large contraptions rigged to their bows were acoustic sweeps, used to detect underwater mines. The spire of St John's is in the background.

Wrens outside their billet, *c.* 1940. As in the First World War, the town was inundated with military personnel. These two girls may have been stationed at HMS *Europa*. They were staying at Mr and Mrs Mitchell's house in Oulton Road.

Sergent Frank Robb, King's Own Scottish Borderers, *c.* 1942. Known affectionately as 'Kosbies', the KOSBs arrived in Lowestoft in 1941. Their arrival was interrupted by German aircraft between Pakefield and Kessingland. During their stay in the town they were billeted in Pakefield and Oulton Road. Frank Robb saw active service on the European front and was involved with liberating inmates of German concentration camps. In 1946 he was awarded the British Empire Medal.

The Arcade, London Road North, 1941. Because the town was inadequately defended, bombing attacks were devastating. Lowestoft was also bombed more than any other town of its size on the east coast. This photograph and the following six are by Ford Jenkins, who was the official Ministry of Information photographer in Lowestoft for most of the war.

The same site photographed in 1945, showing the damage caused by repeated bombing between 1941 and 1942. Most of the area between Regent Road and Milton Road was laid to waste. This site is now part of Westgates.

Till Road and Raglan Street, *c.* 1941. Air-raid shelters nestle in the remains of a bombed-out warehouse. The greengrocer's on the corner was destroyed in 1942.

Standing defiantly in the background is the Church of Our Lady of the Sea in Gordon Road; in the foreground lies the collapsed frontage of Woolworths in London Road North, 1941.

Royal Avenue, 1941. The houses were damaged by small-calibre bombs.

The flags are out for peace, 1945. Many buildings had to be reconstructed, such as Watson's Garage in the High Street, which was damaged in May 1943.

London Road North, showing the shell of Woolworths and Timpson's shoe shop, May 1941. Kay's is to the right. These shops were wrecked in a night raid on the town on 5 May. Although completely gutted, after the war the Woolworths building was reconstructed in a style similar to its pre-war design.

CLIFF EROSION

Children play at the foot of Pakefield Street, May 1930. A hopeful little boy stands behind the girls with his toy yacht. The row of reeds being washed by the tide are the remains of a traditional method of breakwater. However, these were quickly dispersed by the action of the tide.

Pakefield, looking towards the rectory and manor-house, November 1901. Erosion by the sea has plagued this part of the coast for centuries. After a period of relative calm for much of the nineteenth century, problems arose in around 1900, when parts of Pakefield became greatly undermined by the sea. Only a few months after this photograph was taken, the steps leading from the manor-house to the beach collapsed.

Sea encroachment at Pakefield, mid-1930s. Today the sea still bites deep into the cliffs, putting all in peril.

Cliff Road, also known as The Avenue, February 1925. These houses were built in about 1880, when the seas appeared docile.

Cliff Road, later the same year. The sea threatened the two houses nearest to the cliff edge. Attempts were made to salvage as much as possible and recycle the building materials before the erosion reached the houses.

The rear of Cliff Road as it awaited its fate, March 1929.

Cliff Road, September 1930. The last three houses were soon to collapse into the sea, despite attempts to control the forces of nature by erecting concrete defences on the beach.

Cliff Road, summer 1930. Until Pakefield became part of the Borough of Lowestoft in 1934, it was impossible for the village to find the resources to control the impending disaster. Like all catastrophes it became an attraction for sightseers. Also watching the houses unceremoniously falling into the sea was a certain Ernest Graystone, who took this photograph.

All Saints' St Margaret's Church, Pakefield, 1930. Originally this was two churches in one; one side was dedicated to All Saints and the other to St Margaret. The photograph was taken at the cliff edge by an amateur. Eventually the sea reached the confines of the churchyard.

On the beach at the foot of Cliff Road, looking towards Beach Stone Place, September 1930. These concrete defences were an attempt to minimize the effect of the waves.

Beach Stone Place, looking towards what had been the green and the manor-house, 1930. On the beach can be seen the remains of the earlier attempts to arrest the erosion. They had not proved successful, as it had not been taken into account that the sea would go around the defences and undermine the cliffs.

Beach Stone Place from the seashore, 1930. Colby's Café (centre right) is on the edge. The house on the left featured in a startling series of photographs.

The demise of Beach Stone Place, vividly recorded in 1936 by Ernest Graystone. Apprehensive workmen keep an eye on the approaching calamity.

Beach Stone Place, December 1936. The pounding sea sends the first part plunging down.

The rough seas pounded away at the cliff. The building shuddered, and with a roar it crashed into the water, giving young Ernest one of his most famous photographs.

The aftermath. The Jubilee Wall in the background reached this point in 1938, but it was too late to save Beach Stone Place.

Pakefield Street, 1930. Workmen prepare to erect fencing at the top of the cliff. The 'Jolly Sailors', far right, became dangerously close to the edge. It was saved, but it was a very close call.

Kirkley Cliff, November 1903. By September 1903 Kirkley was also threatened by the sea as part of the cliff fell down on to the beach. The behaviour of the sea at this point was blamed on the construction of the newly opened Claremont Pier, from where this photograph was taken. The pier affected the tidal flow just south of the pier.

The coastguard station and cottages, Corton, 1930. Like Pakefield, this village has suffered from coastal erosion. Much land has surrended to the sea over the centuries, and by 1930 the waves had reached the precincts of the gardens of these houses.

The same buildings later that year. Part of the outhouse has gone, and the rest was to follow. On the shore are the remains of a previous attempt at sea defence, built by Russell J. Colman to protect his house, The Clyffe.

Kessingland, 30 January 1937. After many years of wide and pleasant beaches, ferocious storms battered the beach village of Kessingland, washing away the sand. After the storm, cottages on the cliff were at the mercy of the sea; the lifeboat station was a smashed wreck.

Shepherd's Villas, Kessingland, 1937. Traditional attempts at defending the village did not succeed and houses continued to tumble on to the beach. In the following year there were signs that the sea might break through and flood the low-lying countryside around Kessingland.

Section Seven

VILLAGES

Pakefield lifeboat, 1869. Taken from Pakefield Score, this early photograph shows the inauguration of the Pakefield number two lifeboat. The design of this vessel was similar to that of Lowestoft's first offical lifeboat the Francis Ann, *launched in 1807. As far as can be ascertained, this is the oldest surviving photograph of a Pakefield lifeboat.*

Mutford Lock and the village of Oulton Broad, showing the old Wherry Inn, *c.* 1890. The lock was built in 1828, while a bridge has been here since the seventeenth century. On part of the original waterway to Norwich, it stands at the point where Lake Lothing meets the Broads. The large windmill in Bridge Road was demolished in 1937.

The Wherry Inn, Mutford Lock, *c.* 1896. Here it is about to be pulled down to make way for the present, grand Wherry Hotel.

Bridge Road, Oulton Broad, photographed from the Wherry Hotel, *c*. 1930. The village of Oulton Broad comprises the parishes of Carlton Colville and Oulton, situated around Mutford Lock and the Oulton Broad, from which it gets its name. The photograph is taken from the Carlton Colville side. During the last century the Broads became a great favourite with the yachting fraternity and the village expanded accordingly. The bridge over the lock (bottom left) was built in 1894 and was replaced in 1937 by a wider, more appropriate structure for carrying motor traffic. Oulton Broad became part of Lowestoft in 1919.

St Michael's Church, Oulton, 1860s. It was originally built in the shape of a crucifix, and once belonged to the Fastolf family, who owned large areas of Oulton in the fifteenth century. John Fastolf, who died in 1445, is buried here.

The interior of St Michael's, *c.* 1908. Much of the building dates from the early Norman period, including this fine archway. Standing under it is the churchwarden, who is holding the bellrope. The organ was located in an alcove at the base of the tower. The object which looks like a gramophone horn is in fact a megaphone; this was needed to project the curate's voice to all parts of the church.

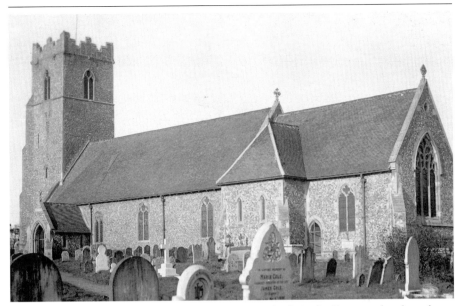

St. Peter's Church, Carlton Colville, c. 1912. It was built in the Decorated style and was restored in 1883. At the time of this photograph the church had five bells. Revd Reginald Augustus Bignold was the rector from 1898 until his death in 1944.

A pastoral play, Carlton Colville, August 1910. Children from St Peter's End School are photographed on the rectory lawn. The play was written by their headmaster, Mr B.J. Quadling.

The main entrance to Somerleyton Hall, early 1860s. Though dating back to the Elizabethan period, the house was rebuilt in the 1840s in the Italianate style. At the time of this photograph it was the home of Sir Morton Peto. However, financial problems forced him to sell the house to Sir Francis Crossley in 1863.

A magnificent view of the house in about 1865, with its domed rotunda winter gardens, inspired by Paxton's Crystal Palace. Regrettably the rotunda was demolished many years ago.

Somerleyton, *c.* 1912. This 'model village' was begun by Sir Morton Peto and completed by the Crossleys. It is a pretty little village, full of thatched cottages located around a pleasant green. Beyond the signpost is the village school. The road to the right leads to Lowestoft.

Herringfleet School, *c.* 1906. Situated on the road from Somerleyton to St Olave's, it was a mixed boys' and girls' school. At the time of this photograph, it was run by the County Council. It closed in 1909.

Threshing time on the Somerleyton estate during the Edwardian era. Men and boys all helped with the gathering of the harvest. For the children it meant no school, which they obviously did not mind. Despite advances in technology, harvesting was still a labour-intensive job.

A quiet country lane near Blundestone, *c.* 1904. Apart from the telegraph pole, this scene would have been very much the same when Dickens visited the village in the 1840s, seeking material for *David Copperfield*.

Corton church and Church Farm, 1860s. For many years most of this church was a ruin, and only a small part of it was used for services. It originally served a much larger community stretching as far as the long-lost village of Newton, now under the North Sea. The body of the church was restored and extended in the 1980s, but the tower is still in a state of decay.

Corton, c. 1904. A flagpole stands outside the post office. In the last half of the nineteenth century the Colmans of Norwich did much to improve the old village, building many of the cottages, which can still be seen today.

St Michael's Church, Rushmere, *c.* 1912. Located on the Carlton Colville road, it once stood proud, but later became derelict.

The church of St John the Baptist, Barnaby, *c.* 1912. Located on the Beccles to Lowestoft road, it was restored in 1882 at a cost of £250 and seated 90 parishioners.

A Wolseley attempts to breach the flood at Latymer's Dam, Kessingland, 1938. The sea broke through and flooded a large area around the village. The catastrophe had been expected since the previous year, when Kessingland had lost most of its beach.

The office and reception at Kessingland Holiday Camp, 1938. The camp was originally Kessingland Grange Girls' School, but by 1933 it had become a holiday camp, run by George Catchpole. The sender of this postcard complains of paying 2d for a bar of chocolate and moans about the quality of the orangeade.

Acknowledgements

I am indebted to my good friend Jack Rose, to members of the Jack Rose Old Lowestoft Society and to those kind individuals who have assisted me by sharing information and personal memories. I am very grateful to David White, who allowed me access to material relating to the early days of scouting in Lowestoft. Special thanks are due to Miss Kate Chantry of the Suffolk Record Office for her kind help and advice, as is a special acknowledgement to Ernest Graystone, without whose photographic work the town of Lowestoft would be very much the poorer. I owe a debt of thanks for permission to reproduce photographs on the following pages:

Ernest Graystone, 59, 66, 68, (top), 71, 107, 110 (both), 111 (both); Miss Ann Hubbard, 53 (bottom), 58 (bottom), 122 (bottom); Ford Jenkins Ltd, 69, 99, (both), 100 (both), 101 (both), 102; 14th Lowestoft Scout Group, 83 (bottom), 84 (both); Ian Mitchell, 41 (top), 98 (top); Peter Mitchell, 27 (bottom), 85 (top); Mrs Joan Plant, 4, 82, (bottom), 91 (bottom); Sidney Reynolds, 18, 19, 23 (both), 24 (both); Jack Rose, 41 (bottom); Suffolk Record Office, Lowestoft, 15 (ES 178/7/1), 16 (ES 178/7/1), 17 (PH-S/STR/100) (top) and (PH-S/STR/95) (bottom), 21 (PH-S/STR/31a) (top) and (PH-L/TRA/6) (bottom), 26 (PH-L/STR/57) (bottom), 28 (PH-L/TRA/5) (top), 75 (PH-S/PER/26); Bob Taylor, 11 (both), 37 (top), 38 (both), 123 (bottom); Trevor Westgate; 2, 31, 44 (top), 45 (top), 51 (bottom), 74 (top), 79, 88.

All other material comes from my own archive. Therefore, I must acknowledge a final debt of gratitude to all of those photographers over the years, professional and amateur, known and unknown, without whom this book and my archive would not exist.

BRITAIN IN OLD PHOTOGRAPHS

To order any of these titles please telephone Littlehampton Book services 01903 721596

ALDERNEY

Alderney: A Second Selection, *B Bonnard*

BEDFORDSHIRE

Bedfordshire at Work, *N Lutt*

BERKSHIRE

Maidenhead, *M Hayles & D Hedges*
Around Maidenhead, *M Hayles & B Hedges*
Reading, *P Southerton*
Reading: A Second Selection, *P Southerton*
Sandhurst and Crowthorne, *K Dancy*
Around Slough, *J Hunter & K Hunter*
Around Thatcham, *P Allen*
Around Windsor, *B Hedges*

BUCKINGHAMSHIRE

Buckingham and District, *R Cook*
High Wycombe, *R Goodearl*
Around Stony Stratford, *A Lambert*

CHESHIRE

Cheshire Railways, *M Hitches*
Chester, *S Nichols*

CLWYD

Clwyd Railways, *M Hitches*

CLYDESDALE

Clydesdale, *Lesmahagow Parish Historical Association*

CORNWALL

Cornish Coast, *T Bowden*
Falmouth, *P Gilson*
Lower Fal, *P Gilson*
Around Padstow, *M McCarthy*
Around Penzance, *J Holmes*
Penzance and Newlyn, *J Holmes*
Around Truro, *A Lyne*
Upper Fal, *P Gilson*

CUMBERLAND

Cockermouth and District, *J Bernard Bradbury*
Keswick and the Central Lakes, *J Marsh*
Around Penrith, *F Boyd*
Around Whitehaven, *H Fancy*

DERBYSHIRE

Derby, *D Buxton*
Around Matlock, *D Barton*

DEVON

Colyton and Seaton, *T Gosling*
Dawlish and Teignmouth, *G Gosling*
Devon Aerodromes, *K Saunders*
Exeter, *P Thomas*
Exmouth and Budleigh Salterton, *T Gosling*
From Haldon to Mid-Dartmoor, *T Hall*
Honiton and the Otter Valley, *J Yallop*
Around Kingsbridge, *K Tanner*
Around Seaton and Sidmouth, *T Gosling*
Seaton, Axminster and Lyme Regis, *T Gosling*

DORSET

Around Blandford Forum, *B Cox*
Bournemouth, *M Colman*
Bridport and the Bride Valley, *J Burrell & S Humphries*
Dorchester, *T Gosling*
Around Gillingham, *P Crocker*

DURHAM

Darlington, *G Flynn*
Darlington: A Second Selection, *G Flynn*
Durham People, *M Richardson*
Houghton-le-Spring and Hetton-le-Hole, *K Richardson*
Houghton-le-Spring and Hetton-le-Hole:
  A Second Selection, *K Richardson*
Sunderland, *S Miller & B Bell*
Teesdale, *D Coggins*
Teesdale: A Second Selection, *P Raine*
Weardale, *J Crosby*
Weardale: A Second Selection, *J Crosby*

DYFED

Aberystwyth and North Ceredigion,
  Dyfed Cultural Services Dept
Haverfordwest, *Dyfed Cultural Services Dept*
Upper Tywi Valley, *Dyfed Cultural Services Dept*

ESSEX

Around Grays, *B Evans*

GLOUCESTERSHIRE

Along the Avon from Stratford to Tewkesbury, *J Jeremiah*
Cheltenham: A Second Selection, *R Whiting*
Cheltenham at War, *P Gill*
Cirencester, *J Welsford*
Around Cirencester, *E Cuss & P Griffiths*
Forest, The, *D Mullin*
Gloucester, *J Voyce*
Around Gloucester, *A Sutton*
Gloucester: From the Walwin Collection, *J Voyce*
North Cotswolds, *D Viner*
Severn Vale, *A Sutton*
Stonehouse to Painswick, *A Sutton*
Stroud and the Five Valleys, *S Gardiner & L Padin*
Stroud and the Five Valleys: A Second Selection,
  S Gardiner & L Padin
Stroud's Golden Valley, *S Gardiner & L Padin*
Stroudwater and Thames & Severn Canals,
  E Cuss & S Gardiner
Stroudwater and Thames & Severn Canals: A Second
  Selection, *E Cuss & S Gardiner*
Tewkesbury and the Vale of Gloucester, *C Hilton*
Thornbury to Berkeley, *J Hudson*
Uley, Dursley and Cam, *A Sutton*
Wotton-under-Edge to Chipping Sodbury, *A Sutton*

GWYNEDD

Anglesey, *M Hitches*
Gwynedd Railways, *M Hitches*
Around Llandudno, *M Hitches*
Vale of Conwy, *M Hitches*

HAMPSHIRE

Gosport, *J Sadden*
Portsmouth, *P Rogers & D Francis*

HEREFORDSHIRE

Herefordshire, *A Sandford*

HERTFORDSHIRE

Barnet, *I Norrie*
Hitchin, *A Fleck*
St Albans, *S Mullins*
Stevenage, *M Appleton*

ISLE OF MAN

The Tourist Trophy, *B Snelling*

ISLE OF WIGHT

Newport, *D Parr*
Around Ryde, *D Parr*

JERSEY

Jersey: A Third Selection, *R Lemprière*

KENT

Bexley, *M Scott*
Broadstairs and St Peter's, *J Whyman*
Bromley, Keston and Hayes, *M Scott*
Canterbury: A Second Selection, *D Butler*
Chatham and Gillingham, *P MacDougall*
Chatham Dockyard, *P MacDougall*
Deal, *J Broady*
Early Broadstairs and St Peter's, *B Wootton*
East Kent at War, *D Collyer*
Eltham, *J Kennett*
Folkestone: A Second Selection, *A Taylor & E Rooney*
Goudhurst to Tenterden, *A Guilmant*
Gravesend, *R Hiscock*
Around Gravesham, *R Hiscock & D Grierson*
Herne Bay, *J Hawkins*
Lympne Airport, *D Collyer*
Maidstone, *I Hales*
Margate, *R Clements*
RAF Hawkinge, *R Humphreys*
RAF Manston, *RAF Manston History Club*
RAF Manston: A Second Selection,
  RAF Manston History Club
Ramsgate and Thanet Life, *D Perkins*
Romney Marsh, *E Carpenter*
Sandwich, *C Wanostrocht*
Around Tonbridge, *C Bell*
Tunbridge Wells, *M Rowlands & I Beavis*
Tunbridge Wells: A Second Selection,
  M Rowlands & I Beavis
Around Whitstable, *C Court*
Wingham, Adisham and Littlebourne, *M Crane*

LANCASHIRE

Around Barrow-in-Furness, *J Garbutt & J Marsh*
Blackpool, *C Rothwell*
Bury, *J Hudson*
Chorley and District, *J Smith*
Fleetwood, *C Rothwell*
Heywood, *J Hudson*
Around Kirkham, *C Rothwell*
Lancashire North of the Sands, *J Garbutt & J Marsh*
Around Lancaster, *S Ashworth*
Lytham St Anne's, *C Rothwell*
North Fylde, *C Rothwell*
Radcliffe, *J Hudson*
Rossendale, *B Moore & N Dunnachie*

LEICESTERSHIRE

Around Ashby-de-la-Zouch, *K Hillier*
Charnwood Forest, *I Keil, W Humphrey & D Wix*
Leicester, *D Burton*
Leicester: A Second Selection, *D Burton*
Melton Mowbray, *T Hickman*
Around Melton Mowbray, *T Hickman*
River Soar, *D Wix, P Shacklock & I Keil*
Rutland, *T Clough*
Vale of Belvoir, *T Hickman*
Around the Welland Valley, *S Mastoris*

LINCOLNSHIRE

Grimsby, *J Tierney*
Around Grimsby, *J Tierney*
Grimsby Docks, *J Tierney*
Lincoln, *D Cuppleditch*